DON'T QUIT

PERSONAL TRAINING CLIENT LOG BOOK

CONTENTS

APPENDIX

CLIENT DETAILS

Client Name:
Address:
Postcode:
Email:
Phone:
Medical Information:
Aches / Pain / Injuries:
Goals:

EMERGENCY CONTACT DETAILS

Name:
Email: Phone:
Relationship to Client:

PAR-Q

PHYSICAL ACTIVITY READINESS QUESTIONNAIRE

If you are between the ages of 15 and 69, this questionnaire will advise you if you should check with your doctor before any changes to your physical activity routine. If you over 69 years of ages and not active, please check with your doctor before commencing any personal training.

	YES	NO
1. Have you ever been advised by your doctor that you have a heart condition and should only do physical activity recommended by a doctor?	☐	☐
2. Do you feel pain in your chest when you do physical activity?	☐	☐
3. Have you had chest pain in the last 6 months when you were not doing physical activity?	☐	☐
4. Do you ever feel faint or lose balance because of dizziness?	☐	☐
5. Do you have a bone or joint problem which could be made worse doing physical exercise?	☐	☐
6. Do you suffer from high blood pressure?	☐	☐
7. Are you currently taking any medication? If answer "yes" please state medication:	☐	☐
8. Is there any other reason why you should not participate in physical activity? If answer "yes" please explain why:	☐	☐

If you have answered "YES" to one or more of the above questions please talk to you doctor to make sure it is safe for you to become physically active.

If you have answered "NO" to all of the above questions it is reasonably safe for you to become physically active. Remember to build up your fitness gradually.

☐ **I have read and understand the PAR-Q**

Signature [＿＿＿＿＿＿] Print Name [＿＿＿＿＿＿] Date [＿＿＿]

☐ **Having answered "YES" to one or more of the above questions**, I have sought medical advice and I am allowed to start a new physical activity routine.

Signature [＿＿＿＿＿＿] Print Name [＿＿＿＿＿＿] Date [＿＿＿]

CLIENT ASSESSMENT

DOB / AGE		HEIGHT		MAX HR	

DATE								
RESTING HEART RATE (BPM)								
BLOOD PRESSURE (MMHG)								
BODY MASS INDEX (BMI)								
BODY WEIGHT								
BODY COMPOSITION (%)								
Fat								
Visceral Fat								
Muscle								
BODY MEASUREMENTS (MM)								
Chest								
Upper Arms								
Thighs								
Waist								
Hips								
Waist / Hip Ratio								
SKIN FOLD MEASUREMENTS (MM)								
Bicep								
Tricep								
Subscapular								
Supra Iliac								
Total mm								
Fat %								

FITNESS TESTING

DATE								
CARDIO								
Balke Treadmill								
Cooper 2.4km/1.5mile Run								
Cooper 4.8km/3mile Walk								
VO2 Max								
STRENGTH ENDURANCE (NUMBER OF REPS / TIME TO FAILURE)								
Plank								
Press Ups								
Sit Ups								
POWER								
Vertical Jump								
Standing Broad Jump								

RANGE OF MOVEMENT (°)

	Left	Right	Left	Right	Left	Right	Left	Right	Left	Right	Left	Right	Left	Right	Left	Right
Iliopsoas																
Hamstrings																
Quadriceps																
Adductors																
Pectoralis Major																
Latissimus Dorsi																

1-REP MAX (1RM)

DATE									
1RM									
Bicep Curl									
Back Squat									
Bent Over Row									
Chest Press									
Deadlift									
Heel Raise									
Hip Extension									
Hip Flexion									
Lat Pull Down									
Leg Adduction									
Leg Curl									
Leg Extension									
Leg Press									
Low Row									
Military Press									
Overhead Press									
Power Clean									
Seated Row									
Shoulder Press									
Smith Machine Squat									
Split Squat									
Stiff Leg Deadlift									
Tricep Push Down									

SMART GOALS

S SPECIFIC

M MEASURABLE

A ATTAINABLE

R REALISTIC

T TIME-BOUND

12 MONTH PERIODISATION

TRAINING TYPE	MONTH												
Power													
Strength													
Hypertrophy													
Strength Endurance													
Endurance													
Long Slow Duration													
Aerobic Intervals 1:1 - 1:1/2													
Lactate Intervals 1:4 - 1:2													
Creatine Phosphate Intervals 1:6													
Fartlek													

DATE: PT: SESSION NO: PAID: ☐

TRAINING PHASE: E ☐   SE ☐   H ☐   S ☐   P ☐

SESSION:

WARM UP

CARDIOVASCULAR WORKOUT

MAIN SESSION

EXERCISE	WEIGHT	SETS X REPS	REST	NOTES

COOL DOWN

FLEXIBILITY

DATE: PT: SESSION NO: PAID: ☐

TRAINING PHASE: E ☐   SE ☐   H ☐   S ☐   P ☐

SESSION:

WARM UP

CARDIOVASCULAR WORKOUT

MAIN SESSION

EXERCISE	WEIGHT	SETS X REPS	REST	NOTES

COOL DOWN

FLEXIBILITY

DATE: PT: SESSION NO: PAID: ☐

TRAINING PHASE: E ☐ SE ☐ H ☐ S ☐ P ☐

SESSION:

WARM UP

CARDIOVASCULAR WORKOUT

MAIN SESSION

EXERCISE	WEIGHT	SETS X REPS	REST	NOTES

COOL DOWN

FLEXIBILITY

DATE: PT: SESSION NO: PAID: ☐

TRAINING PHASE: E ☐   SE ☐   H ☐   S ☐   P ☐

SESSION:

WARM UP

CARDIOVASCULAR WORKOUT

MAIN SESSION

EXERCISE	WEIGHT	SETS X REPS	REST	NOTES

COOL DOWN

FLEXIBILITY

DATE: PT: SESSION NO: PAID: ☐

TRAINING PHASE: E ☐   SE ☐   H ☐   S ☐   P ☐

SESSION:

WARM UP

CARDIOVASCULAR WORKOUT

MAIN SESSION

EXERCISE	WEIGHT	SETS X REPS	REST	NOTES

COOL DOWN

FLEXIBILITY

DATE: .... PT: .... SESSION NO: .... PAID: ☐

TRAINING PHASE: E ☐ SE ☐ H ☐ S ☐ P ☐

SESSION:

WARM UP

CARDIOVASCULAR WORKOUT

MAIN SESSION

EXERCISE	WEIGHT	SETS X REPS	REST	NOTES

COOL DOWN

FLEXIBILITY

DATE: PT: SESSION NO: PAID: ☐

TRAINING PHASE: E ☐   SE ☐   H ☐   S ☐   P ☐

SESSION:

WARM UP

CARDIOVASCULAR WORKOUT

MAIN SESSION

EXERCISE	WEIGHT	SETS X REPS	REST	NOTES

COOL DOWN

FLEXIBILITY

DATE: PT: SESSION NO: PAID: ☐

TRAINING PHASE: E ☐   SE ☐   H ☐   S ☐   P ☐

SESSION:

WARM UP

CARDIOVASCULAR WORKOUT

MAIN SESSION

EXERCISE	WEIGHT	SETS X REPS	REST	NOTES

COOL DOWN

FLEXIBILITY

DATE: PT: SESSION NO: PAID: ☐

TRAINING PHASE: E ☐ SE ☐ H ☐ S ☐ P ☐

SESSION:

WARM UP

CARDIOVASCULAR WORKOUT

MAIN SESSION

EXERCISE	WEIGHT	SETS X REPS	REST	NOTES

COOL DOWN

FLEXIBILITY

DATE: PT: SESSION NO: PAID: ☐

TRAINING PHASE: E ☐   SE ☐   H ☐   S ☐   P ☐

SESSION:

WARM UP

CARDIOVASCULAR WORKOUT

MAIN SESSION

EXERCISE	WEIGHT	SETS X REPS	REST	NOTES

COOL DOWN

FLEXIBILITY

DATE: PT: SESSION NO: PAID: ☐

TRAINING PHASE: E ☐   SE ☐   H ☐   S ☐   P ☐

SESSION:

WARM UP

CARDIOVASCULAR WORKOUT

MAIN SESSION

EXERCISE	WEIGHT	SETS X REPS	REST	NOTES

COOL DOWN

FLEXIBILITY

DATE: PT: SESSION NO: PAID: ☐

TRAINING PHASE: E ☐ SE ☐ H ☐ S ☐ P ☐

SESSION:

WARM UP

CARDIOVASCULAR WORKOUT

MAIN SESSION

EXERCISE	WEIGHT	SETS X REPS	REST	NOTES

COOL DOWN

FLEXIBILITY

DATE: PT: SESSION NO: PAID: ☐

TRAINING PHASE: E ☐   SE ☐   H ☐   S ☐   P ☐

SESSION:

WARM UP

CARDIOVASCULAR WORKOUT

MAIN SESSION

EXERCISE	WEIGHT	SETS X REPS	REST	NOTES

COOL DOWN

FLEXIBILITY

DATE: PT: SESSION NO: PAID: ☐

TRAINING PHASE: E ☐ SE ☐ H ☐ S ☐ P ☐

SESSION:

WARM UP

CARDIOVASCULAR WORKOUT

MAIN SESSION

EXERCISE	WEIGHT	SETS X REPS	REST	NOTES

COOL DOWN

FLEXIBILITY

DATE: PT: SESSION NO: PAID: ☐

TRAINING PHASE: E ☐ SE ☐ H ☐ S ☐ P ☐

SESSION:

WARM UP

CARDIOVASCULAR WORKOUT

MAIN SESSION

EXERCISE	WEIGHT	SETS X REPS	REST	NOTES

COOL DOWN

FLEXIBILITY

DATE: PT: SESSION NO: PAID: ☐

TRAINING PHASE: E ☐   SE ☐   H ☐   S ☐   P ☐

SESSION:

WARM UP

CARDIOVASCULAR WORKOUT

MAIN SESSION

EXERCISE	WEIGHT	SETS X REPS	REST	NOTES

COOL DOWN

FLEXIBILITY

DATE: PT: SESSION NO: PAID: ☐

TRAINING PHASE: E ☐   SE ☐   H ☐   S ☐   P ☐

SESSION:

WARM UP

CARDIOVASCULAR WORKOUT

MAIN SESSION

EXERCISE	WEIGHT	SETS X REPS	REST	NOTES

COOL DOWN

FLEXIBILITY

DATE: PT: SESSION NO: PAID: ☐

TRAINING PHASE: E ☐ SE ☐ H ☐ S ☐ P ☐

SESSION:

WARM UP

CARDIOVASCULAR WORKOUT

MAIN SESSION

EXERCISE	WEIGHT	SETS X REPS	REST	NOTES

COOL DOWN

FLEXIBILITY

DATE: PT: SESSION NO: PAID: ☐

TRAINING PHASE: E ☐   SE ☐   H ☐   S ☐   P ☐

SESSION:

WARM UP

CARDIOVASCULAR WORKOUT

MAIN SESSION

EXERCISE	WEIGHT	SETS X REPS	REST	NOTES

COOL DOWN

FLEXIBILITY

DATE: PT: SESSION NO: PAID: ☐

TRAINING PHASE: E ☐   SE ☐   H ☐   S ☐   P ☐

SESSION:

WARM UP

CARDIOVASCULAR WORKOUT

MAIN SESSION

EXERCISE	WEIGHT	SETS X REPS	REST	NOTES

COOL DOWN

FLEXIBILITY

DATE: PT: SESSION NO: PAID: ☐

TRAINING PHASE: E ☐ SE ☐ H ☐ S ☐ P ☐

SESSION:

WARM UP

CARDIOVASCULAR WORKOUT

MAIN SESSION

EXERCISE	WEIGHT	SETS X REPS	REST	NOTES

COOL DOWN

FLEXIBILITY

DATE: PT: SESSION NO: PAID: ☐

TRAINING PHASE: E ☐   SE ☐   H ☐   S ☐   P ☐

SESSION:

WARM UP

CARDIOVASCULAR WORKOUT

MAIN SESSION

EXERCISE	WEIGHT	SETS X REPS	REST	NOTES

COOL DOWN

FLEXIBILITY

DATE: .... PT: .... SESSION NO: .... PAID: ☐

TRAINING PHASE: E ☐   SE ☐   H ☐   S ☐   P ☐

SESSION:

WARM UP

CARDIOVASCULAR WORKOUT

MAIN SESSION

EXERCISE	WEIGHT	SETS X REPS	REST	NOTES

COOL DOWN

FLEXIBILITY

DATE: .... PT: SESSION NO: PAID: ☐

TRAINING PHASE: E ☐ SE ☐ H ☐ S ☐ P ☐

SESSION:

WARM UP

CARDIOVASCULAR WORKOUT

MAIN SESSION

EXERCISE	WEIGHT	SETS X REPS	REST	NOTES

COOL DOWN

FLEXIBILITY

DATE: PT: SESSION NO: PAID: ☐

TRAINING PHASE: E ☐ SE ☐ H ☐ S ☐ P ☐

SESSION:

WARM UP

CARDIOVASCULAR WORKOUT

MAIN SESSION

EXERCISE	WEIGHT	SETS X REPS	REST	NOTES

COOL DOWN

FLEXIBILITY

DATE: PT: SESSION NO: PAID: ☐

TRAINING PHASE: E ☐   SE ☐   H ☐   S ☐   P ☐

SESSION:

WARM UP

CARDIOVASCULAR WORKOUT

MAIN SESSION

EXERCISE	WEIGHT	SETS X REPS	REST	NOTES

COOL DOWN

FLEXIBILITY

DATE: PT: SESSION NO: PAID: ☐

TRAINING PHASE: E ☐ SE ☐ H ☐ S ☐ P ☐

SESSION:

WARM UP

CARDIOVASCULAR WORKOUT

MAIN SESSION

EXERCISE	WEIGHT	SETS X REPS	REST	NOTES

COOL DOWN

FLEXIBILITY

DATE: PT: SESSION NO: PAID: ☐

TRAINING PHASE: E ☐ SE ☐ H ☐ S ☐ P ☐

SESSION:

WARM UP

CARDIOVASCULAR WORKOUT

MAIN SESSION

EXERCISE	WEIGHT	SETS X REPS	REST	NOTES

COOL DOWN

FLEXIBILITY

DATE: PT: SESSION NO: PAID: ☐

TRAINING PHASE: E ☐   SE ☐   H ☐   S ☐   P ☐

SESSION:

WARM UP

CARDIOVASCULAR WORKOUT

MAIN SESSION

EXERCISE	WEIGHT	SETS X REPS	REST	NOTES

COOL DOWN

FLEXIBILITY

DATE: PT: SESSION NO: PAID: ☐

TRAINING PHASE: E ☐   SE ☐   H ☐   S ☐   P ☐

SESSION:

WARM UP

CARDIOVASCULAR WORKOUT

MAIN SESSION

EXERCISE	WEIGHT	SETS X REPS	REST	NOTES

COOL DOWN

FLEXIBILITY

DATE: PT: SESSION NO: PAID: ☐

TRAINING PHASE: E ☐   SE ☐   H ☐   S ☐   P ☐

SESSION:

WARM UP

CARDIOVASCULAR WORKOUT

MAIN SESSION

EXERCISE	WEIGHT	SETS X REPS	REST	NOTES

COOL DOWN

FLEXIBILITY

DATE: PT: SESSION NO: PAID: ☐

TRAINING PHASE: E ☐   SE ☐   H ☐   S ☐   P ☐

SESSION:

WARM UP

CARDIOVASCULAR WORKOUT

MAIN SESSION

EXERCISE	WEIGHT	SETS X REPS	REST	NOTES

COOL DOWN

FLEXIBILITY

DATE: PT: SESSION NO: PAID: ☐

TRAINING PHASE: E ☐   SE ☐   H ☐   S ☐   P ☐

SESSION:

WARM UP

CARDIOVASCULAR WORKOUT

MAIN SESSION

EXERCISE	WEIGHT	SETS X REPS	REST	NOTES

COOL DOWN

FLEXIBILITY

DATE: PT: SESSION NO: PAID: ☐

TRAINING PHASE: E ☐ SE ☐ H ☐ S ☐ P ☐

SESSION:

WARM UP

CARDIOVASCULAR WORKOUT

MAIN SESSION

EXERCISE	WEIGHT	SETS X REPS	REST	NOTES

COOL DOWN

FLEXIBILITY

DATE: PT: SESSION NO: PAID: ☐

TRAINING PHASE: E ☐   SE ☐   H ☐   S ☐   P ☐

SESSION:

WARM UP

CARDIOVASCULAR WORKOUT

MAIN SESSION

EXERCISE	WEIGHT	SETS X REPS	REST	NOTES

COOL DOWN

FLEXIBILITY

DATE: PT: SESSION NO: PAID: ☐

TRAINING PHASE: E ☐ SE ☐ H ☐ S ☐ P ☐

SESSION:

WARM UP

CARDIOVASCULAR WORKOUT

MAIN SESSION

EXERCISE	WEIGHT	SETS X REPS	REST	NOTES

COOL DOWN

FLEXIBILITY

DATE: PT: SESSION NO: PAID: ☐

TRAINING PHASE: E ☐ SE ☐ H ☐ S ☐ P ☐

SESSION:

WARM UP

CARDIOVASCULAR WORKOUT

MAIN SESSION

EXERCISE	WEIGHT	SETS X REPS	REST	NOTES

COOL DOWN

FLEXIBILITY

DATE: PT: SESSION NO: PAID: ☐

TRAINING PHASE: E ☐ SE ☐ H ☐ S ☐ P ☐

SESSION:

WARM UP

CARDIOVASCULAR WORKOUT

MAIN SESSION

EXERCISE	WEIGHT	SETS X REPS	REST	NOTES

COOL DOWN

FLEXIBILITY

DATE: PT: SESSION NO: PAID: ☐

TRAINING PHASE: E ☐ SE ☐ H ☐ S ☐ P ☐

SESSION:

WARM UP

CARDIOVASCULAR WORKOUT

MAIN SESSION

EXERCISE	WEIGHT	SETS X REPS	REST	NOTES

COOL DOWN

FLEXIBILITY

DATE: PT: SESSION NO: PAID: ☐

TRAINING PHASE: E ☐ SE ☐ H ☐ S ☐ P ☐

SESSION:

WARM UP

CARDIOVASCULAR WORKOUT

MAIN SESSION

EXERCISE	WEIGHT	SETS X REPS	REST	NOTES

COOL DOWN

FLEXIBILITY

DATE: PT: SESSION NO: PAID: ☐

TRAINING PHASE: E ☐   SE ☐   H ☐   S ☐   P ☐

SESSION:

WARM UP

CARDIOVASCULAR WORKOUT

MAIN SESSION

EXERCISE	WEIGHT	SETS X REPS	REST	NOTES

COOL DOWN

FLEXIBILITY

DATE: PT: SESSION NO: PAID: ☐

TRAINING PHASE: E ☐ SE ☐ H ☐ S ☐ P ☐

SESSION:

WARM UP

CARDIOVASCULAR WORKOUT

MAIN SESSION

EXERCISE	WEIGHT	SETS X REPS	REST	NOTES

COOL DOWN

FLEXIBILITY

DATE: PT: SESSION NO: PAID: ☐

TRAINING PHASE: E ☐   SE ☐   H ☐   S ☐   P ☐

SESSION:

WARM UP

CARDIOVASCULAR WORKOUT

MAIN SESSION

EXERCISE	WEIGHT	SETS X REPS	REST	NOTES

COOL DOWN

FLEXIBILITY

DATE: PT: SESSION NO: PAID: ☐

TRAINING PHASE: E ☐   SE ☐   H ☐   S ☐   P ☐

SESSION:

WARM UP

CARDIOVASCULAR WORKOUT

MAIN SESSION

EXERCISE	WEIGHT	SETS X REPS	REST	NOTES

COOL DOWN

FLEXIBILITY

DATE: PT: SESSION NO: PAID: ☐

TRAINING PHASE: E ☐   SE ☐   H ☐   S ☐   P ☐

SESSION:

WARM UP

CARDIOVASCULAR WORKOUT

MAIN SESSION

EXERCISE	WEIGHT	SETS X REPS	REST	NOTES

COOL DOWN

FLEXIBILITY

DATE: PT: SESSION NO: PAID: ☐

TRAINING PHASE: E ☐   SE ☐   H ☐   S ☐   P ☐

SESSION:

WARM UP

CARDIOVASCULAR WORKOUT

MAIN SESSION

EXERCISE	WEIGHT	SETS X REPS	REST	NOTES

COOL DOWN

FLEXIBILITY

DATE: PT: SESSION NO: PAID: ☐

TRAINING PHASE: E ☐ SE ☐ H ☐ S ☐ P ☐

SESSION:

WARM UP

CARDIOVASCULAR WORKOUT

MAIN SESSION

EXERCISE	WEIGHT	SETS X REPS	REST	NOTES

COOL DOWN

FLEXIBILITY

DATE: PT: SESSION NO: PAID: ☐

TRAINING PHASE: E ☐   SE ☐   H ☐   S ☐   P ☐

SESSION:

WARM UP

CARDIOVASCULAR WORKOUT

MAIN SESSION

EXERCISE	WEIGHT	SETS X REPS	REST	NOTES

COOL DOWN

FLEXIBILITY

DATE: PT: SESSION NO: PAID: ☐

TRAINING PHASE: E ☐   SE ☐   H ☐   S ☐   P ☐

SESSION:

WARM UP

CARDIOVASCULAR WORKOUT

MAIN SESSION

EXERCISE	WEIGHT	SETS X REPS	REST	NOTES

COOL DOWN

FLEXIBILITY

DATE: PT: SESSION NO: PAID: ☐

TRAINING PHASE: E ☐ SE ☐ H ☐ S ☐ P ☐

SESSION:

WARM UP

CARDIOVASCULAR WORKOUT

MAIN SESSION

EXERCISE	WEIGHT	SETS X REPS	REST	NOTES

COOL DOWN

FLEXIBILITY

DATE: .... PT: SESSION NO: PAID: ☐

TRAINING PHASE: E ☐ SE ☐ H ☐ S ☐ P ☐

SESSION:

WARM UP

CARDIOVASCULAR WORKOUT

MAIN SESSION

EXERCISE	WEIGHT	SETS X REPS	REST	NOTES

COOL DOWN

FLEXIBILITY

DATE: PT: SESSION NO: PAID: ☐

TRAINING PHASE: E ☐   SE ☐   H ☐   S ☐   P ☐

SESSION:

WARM UP

CARDIOVASCULAR WORKOUT

MAIN SESSION

EXERCISE	WEIGHT	SETS X REPS	REST	NOTES

COOL DOWN

FLEXIBILITY

DATE: PT: SESSION NO: PAID: ☐

TRAINING PHASE: E ☐ SE ☐ H ☐ S ☐ P ☐

SESSION:

WARM UP

CARDIOVASCULAR WORKOUT

MAIN SESSION

EXERCISE	WEIGHT	SETS X REPS	REST	NOTES

COOL DOWN

FLEXIBILITY

DATE: PT: SESSION NO: PAID: ☐

TRAINING PHASE: E ☐   SE ☐   H ☐   S ☐   P ☐

SESSION:

WARM UP

CARDIOVASCULAR WORKOUT

MAIN SESSION				
EXERCISE	WEIGHT	SETS X REPS	REST	NOTES

COOL DOWN

FLEXIBILITY

DATE: PT: SESSION NO: PAID: ☐

TRAINING PHASE: E ☐   SE ☐   H ☐   S ☐   P ☐

SESSION:

WARM UP

CARDIOVASCULAR WORKOUT

MAIN SESSION

EXERCISE	WEIGHT	SETS X REPS	REST	NOTES

COOL DOWN

FLEXIBILITY

DATE: PT: SESSION NO: PAID: ☐

TRAINING PHASE: E ☐ SE ☐ H ☐ S ☐ P ☐

SESSION:

WARM UP

CARDIOVASCULAR WORKOUT

MAIN SESSION

EXERCISE	WEIGHT	SETS X REPS	REST	NOTES

COOL DOWN

FLEXIBILITY

DATE: PT: SESSION NO: PAID: ☐

TRAINING PHASE: E ☐ SE ☐ H ☐ S ☐ P ☐

SESSION:

WARM UP

CARDIOVASCULAR WORKOUT

MAIN SESSION

EXERCISE	WEIGHT	SETS X REPS	REST	NOTES

COOL DOWN

FLEXIBILITY

DATE: PT: SESSION NO: PAID: ☐

TRAINING PHASE: E ☐ SE ☐ H ☐ S ☐ P ☐

SESSION:

WARM UP

CARDIOVASCULAR WORKOUT

MAIN SESSION

EXERCISE	WEIGHT	SETS X REPS	REST	NOTES

COOL DOWN

FLEXIBILITY

DATE: PT: SESSION NO: PAID: ☐

TRAINING PHASE: E ☐ SE ☐ H ☐ S ☐ P ☐

SESSION:

WARM UP

CARDIOVASCULAR WORKOUT

MAIN SESSION

EXERCISE	WEIGHT	SETS X REPS	REST	NOTES

COOL DOWN

FLEXIBILITY

TRAINING PHASE: E ☐   SE ☐   H ☐   S ☐   P ☐

SESSION:

WARM UP

CARDIOVASCULAR WORKOUT

MAIN SESSION

EXERCISE	WEIGHT	SETS X REPS	REST	NOTES

COOL DOWN

FLEXIBILITY

TRAINING PHASE: E ☐   SE ☐   H ☐   S ☐   P ☐

SESSION:

WARM UP

CARDIOVASCULAR WORKOUT

MAIN SESSION

EXERCISE	WEIGHT	SETS X REPS	REST	NOTES

COOL DOWN

FLEXIBILITY

DATE: PT: SESSION NO: PAID: ☐

TRAINING PHASE: E ☐ SE ☐ H ☐ S ☐ P ☐

SESSION:

WARM UP

CARDIOVASCULAR WORKOUT

MAIN SESSION

EXERCISE	WEIGHT	SETS X REPS	REST	NOTES

COOL DOWN

FLEXIBILITY

DATE: PT: SESSION NO: PAID: ☐

TRAINING PHASE: E ☐   SE ☐   H ☐   S ☐   P ☐

SESSION:

WARM UP

CARDIOVASCULAR WORKOUT

MAIN SESSION

EXERCISE	WEIGHT	SETS X REPS	REST	NOTES

COOL DOWN

FLEXIBILITY

DATE: PT: SESSION NO: PAID: ☐

TRAINING PHASE: E ☐   SE ☐   H ☐   S ☐   P ☐

SESSION:

WARM UP

CARDIOVASCULAR WORKOUT

MAIN SESSION

EXERCISE	WEIGHT	SETS X REPS	REST	NOTES

COOL DOWN

FLEXIBILITY

DATE: PT: SESSION NO: PAID: ☐

TRAINING PHASE: E ☐   SE ☐   H ☐   S ☐   P ☐

SESSION:

WARM UP

CARDIOVASCULAR WORKOUT

MAIN SESSION

EXERCISE	WEIGHT	SETS X REPS	REST	NOTES

COOL DOWN

FLEXIBILITY

DATE: .... PT: .... SESSION NO: .... PAID: ☐

TRAINING PHASE: E ☐ SE ☐ H ☐ S ☐ P ☐

SESSION:

WARM UP

CARDIOVASCULAR WORKOUT

MAIN SESSION

EXERCISE	WEIGHT	SETS X REPS	REST	NOTES

COOL DOWN

FLEXIBILITY

DATE: PT: SESSION NO: PAID: ☐

TRAINING PHASE: E ☐   SE ☐   H ☐   S ☐   P ☐

SESSION:

WARM UP

CARDIOVASCULAR WORKOUT

MAIN SESSION

EXERCISE	WEIGHT	SETS X REPS	REST	NOTES

COOL DOWN

FLEXIBILITY

DATE: PT: SESSION NO: PAID: ☐

TRAINING PHASE: E ☐   SE ☐   H ☐   S ☐   P ☐

SESSION:

WARM UP

CARDIOVASCULAR WORKOUT

MAIN SESSION

EXERCISE	WEIGHT	SETS X REPS	REST	NOTES

COOL DOWN

FLEXIBILITY

DATE: PT: SESSION NO: PAID: ☐

TRAINING PHASE: E ☐   SE ☐   H ☐   S ☐   P ☐

SESSION:

WARM UP

CARDIOVASCULAR WORKOUT

MAIN SESSION

EXERCISE	WEIGHT	SETS X REPS	REST	NOTES

COOL DOWN

FLEXIBILITY

DATE: PT: SESSION NO: PAID: ☐

TRAINING PHASE: E ☐   SE ☐   H ☐   S ☐   P ☐

SESSION:

WARM UP

CARDIOVASCULAR WORKOUT

MAIN SESSION

EXERCISE	WEIGHT	SETS X REPS	REST	NOTES

COOL DOWN

FLEXIBILITY

DATE: PT: SESSION NO: PAID: ☐

TRAINING PHASE: E ☐ SE ☐ H ☐ S ☐ P ☐

SESSION:

WARM UP

CARDIOVASCULAR WORKOUT

MAIN SESSION

EXERCISE	WEIGHT	SETS X REPS	REST	NOTES

COOL DOWN

FLEXIBILITY

DATE: PT: SESSION NO: PAID: ☐

TRAINING PHASE: E ☐ SE ☐ H ☐ S ☐ P ☐

SESSION:

WARM UP

CARDIOVASCULAR WORKOUT

MAIN SESSION

EXERCISE	WEIGHT	SETS X REPS	REST	NOTES

COOL DOWN

FLEXIBILITY

DATE: PT: SESSION NO: PAID: ☐

TRAINING PHASE: E ☐ SE ☐ H ☐ S ☐ P ☐

SESSION:

WARM UP

CARDIOVASCULAR WORKOUT

MAIN SESSION

EXERCISE	WEIGHT	SETS X REPS	REST	NOTES

COOL DOWN

FLEXIBILITY

DATE: PT: SESSION NO: PAID: ☐

TRAINING PHASE: E ☐   SE ☐   H ☐   S ☐   P ☐

SESSION:

WARM UP

CARDIOVASCULAR WORKOUT

MAIN SESSION

EXERCISE	WEIGHT	SETS X REPS	REST	NOTES

COOL DOWN

FLEXIBILITY

DATE: PT: SESSION NO: PAID: ☐

TRAINING PHASE: E ☐ SE ☐ H ☐ S ☐ P ☐

SESSION:

WARM UP

CARDIOVASCULAR WORKOUT

MAIN SESSION

EXERCISE	WEIGHT	SETS X REPS	REST	NOTES

COOL DOWN

FLEXIBILITY

DATE: PT: SESSION NO: PAID: ☐

TRAINING PHASE: E ☐   SE ☐   H ☐   S ☐   P ☐

SESSION:

WARM UP

CARDIOVASCULAR WORKOUT

MAIN SESSION

EXERCISE	WEIGHT	SETS X REPS	REST	NOTES

COOL DOWN

FLEXIBILITY

DATE: PT: SESSION NO: PAID: ☐

TRAINING PHASE: E ☐   SE ☐   H ☐   S ☐   P ☐

SESSION:

WARM UP

CARDIOVASCULAR WORKOUT

MAIN SESSION

EXERCISE	WEIGHT	SETS X REPS	REST	NOTES

COOL DOWN

FLEXIBILITY

DATE: PT: SESSION NO: PAID: ☐

TRAINING PHASE: E ☐   SE ☐   H ☐   S ☐   P ☐

SESSION:

WARM UP

CARDIOVASCULAR WORKOUT

MAIN SESSION

EXERCISE	WEIGHT	SETS X REPS	REST	NOTES

COOL DOWN

FLEXIBILITY

DATE: PT: SESSION NO: PAID: ☐

TRAINING PHASE: E ☐   SE ☐   H ☐   S ☐   P ☐

SESSION:

WARM UP

CARDIOVASCULAR WORKOUT

MAIN SESSION

EXERCISE	WEIGHT	SETS X REPS	REST	NOTES

COOL DOWN

FLEXIBILITY

DATE: PT: SESSION NO: PAID: ☐

TRAINING PHASE: E ☐   SE ☐   H ☐   S ☐   P ☐

SESSION:

WARM UP

CARDIOVASCULAR WORKOUT

MAIN SESSION

EXERCISE	WEIGHT	SETS X REPS	REST	NOTES

COOL DOWN

FLEXIBILITY

DATE: PT: SESSION NO: PAID: ☐

TRAINING PHASE: E ☐   SE ☐   H ☐   S ☐   P ☐

SESSION:

WARM UP

CARDIOVASCULAR WORKOUT

MAIN SESSION

EXERCISE	WEIGHT	SETS X REPS	REST	NOTES

COOL DOWN

FLEXIBILITY

DATE: PT: SESSION NO: PAID: ☐

TRAINING PHASE: E ☐   SE ☐   H ☐   S ☐   P ☐

SESSION:

WARM UP

CARDIOVASCULAR WORKOUT

MAIN SESSION

EXERCISE	WEIGHT	SETS X REPS	REST	NOTES

COOL DOWN

FLEXIBILITY

DATE: PT: SESSION NO: PAID: ☐

TRAINING PHASE: E ☐   SE ☐   H ☐   S ☐   P ☐

SESSION:

WARM UP

CARDIOVASCULAR WORKOUT

MAIN SESSION

EXERCISE	WEIGHT	SETS X REPS	REST	NOTES

COOL DOWN

FLEXIBILITY

DATE: PT: SESSION NO: PAID: ☐

TRAINING PHASE: E ☐   SE ☐   H ☐   S ☐   P ☐

SESSION:

WARM UP

CARDIOVASCULAR WORKOUT

MAIN SESSION

EXERCISE	WEIGHT	SETS X REPS	REST	NOTES

COOL DOWN

FLEXIBILITY

DATE: PT: SESSION NO: PAID: ☐

TRAINING PHASE: E ☐   SE ☐   H ☐   S ☐   P ☐

SESSION:

WARM UP

CARDIOVASCULAR WORKOUT

MAIN SESSION				
EXERCISE	WEIGHT	SETS X REPS	REST	NOTES

COOL DOWN

FLEXIBILITY

DATE: PT: SESSION NO: PAID: ☐

TRAINING PHASE: E ☐   SE ☐   H ☐   S ☐   P ☐

SESSION:

WARM UP

CARDIOVASCULAR WORKOUT

MAIN SESSION

EXERCISE	WEIGHT	SETS X REPS	REST	NOTES

COOL DOWN

FLEXIBILITY

DATE: PT: SESSION NO: PAID: ☐

TRAINING PHASE: E ☐   SE ☐   H ☐   S ☐   P ☐

SESSION:

WARM UP

CARDIOVASCULAR WORKOUT

MAIN SESSION

EXERCISE	WEIGHT	SETS X REPS	REST	NOTES

COOL DOWN

FLEXIBILITY

DATE: PT: SESSION NO: PAID: [ ]

TRAINING PHASE: E [ ]   SE [ ]   H [ ]   S [ ]   P [ ]

SESSION:

WARM UP

CARDIOVASCULAR WORKOUT

MAIN SESSION

EXERCISE	WEIGHT	SETS X REPS	REST	NOTES

COOL DOWN

FLEXIBILITY

BLOOD PRESSURE CHART

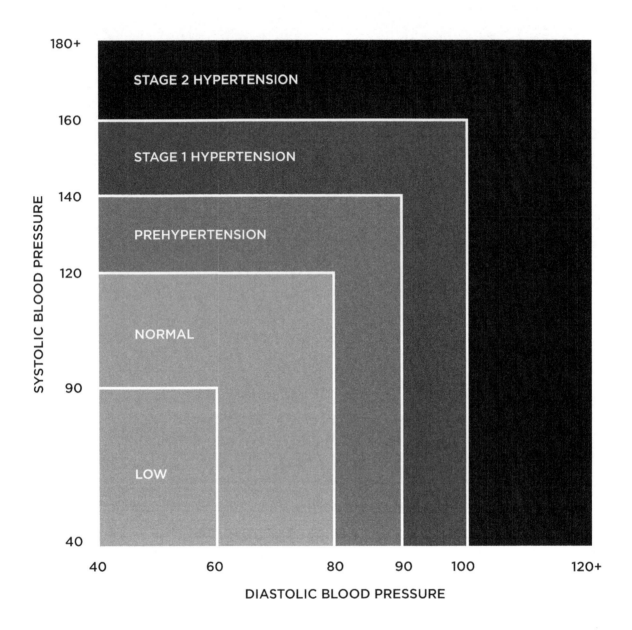

SYSTOLIC BLOOD PRESSURE

180+

STAGE 2 HYPERTENSION

160

STAGE 1 HYPERTENSION

140

PREHYPERTENSION

120

NORMAL

90

LOW

40

40   60   80   90   100   120+

DIASTOLIC BLOOD PRESSURE

BLOOD PRESSURE READINGS

Blood pressure is measured in millimetres of mercury (mmHg) and is given as two figures:

Systolic Pressure – the pressure when your heart pushes blood out

Diastolic Pressure – the pressure when your heart rests between beats

(e.g. 140/90mmHg - systolic pressure of 140mmHg and a diastolic pressure of 90mmHg).

RESTING HEART RATES

RESTING HEART RATE - FEMALE						
AGE	**18-25**	**26-35**	**36-45**	**46-55**	**56-65**	**65+**
ATHLETE	54-60	54-59	54-59	54-60	54-59	54-59
EXCELLENT	61-65	60-64	60-64	61-65	60-64	60-64
GOOD	66-69	65-68	65-69	66-69	65-68	65-68
ABOVE AVERAGE	70-73	69-72	70-73	70-73	69-73	69-72
BELOW AVERAGE	79-84	77-82	79-84	78-83	78-83	77-84
POOR	85+	83+	85+	84+	84+	84+

RESTING HEART RATE - MALE						
AGE	**18-25**	**26-35**	**36-45**	**46-55**	**56-65**	**65+**
ATHLETE	49-55	49-54	50-56	50-57	51-56	50-55
EXCELLENT	56-61	55-61	57-62	58-63	57-61	56-61
GOOD	62-65	62-65	63-66	64-67	62-67	62-65
ABOVE AVERAGE	66-69	66-70	67-70	68-71	68-71	66-69
BELOW AVERAGE	74-81	75-81	76-82	77-83	76-81	74-79
POOR	82+	82+	83+	84+	82+	80+

RESTING HEART RATE

Heart rate readings depend on when it is measured and what you were doing immediately before the reading, so please use this chart as a guide only. The most accurate form of measuring a resting heart rate is after you have been resting for at least 5 minutes.

You heart needs physical activity, so exercise regularly to keep in tip top health.

FRONTAL MUSCLE ANATOMY

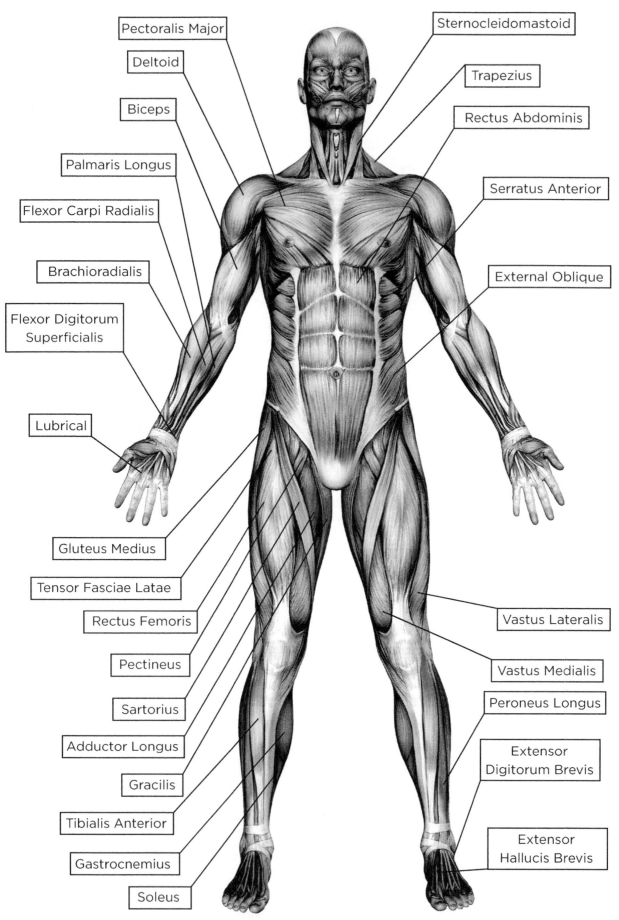

Pectoralis Major

Deltoid

Biceps

Palmaris Longus

Flexor Carpi Radialis

Brachioradialis

Flexor Digitorum Superficialis

Lubrical

Gluteus Medius

Tensor Fasciae Latae

Rectus Femoris

Pectineus

Sartorius

Adductor Longus

Gracilis

Tibialis Anterior

Gastrocnemius

Soleus

Sternocleidomastoid

Trapezius

Rectus Abdominis

Serratus Anterior

External Oblique

Vastus Lateralis

Vastus Medialis

Peroneus Longus

Extensor Digitorum Brevis

Extensor Hallucis Brevis

BACK MUSCLE ANATOMY

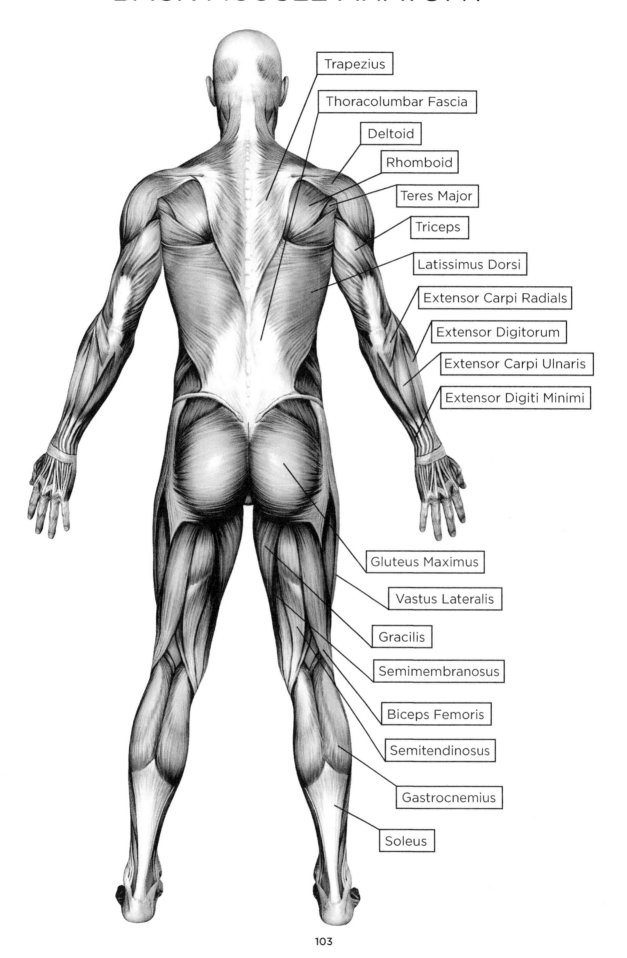

Trapezius

Thoracolumbar Fascia

Deltoid

Rhomboid

Teres Major

Triceps

Latissimus Dorsi

Extensor Carpi Radials

Extensor Digitorum

Extensor Carpi Ulnaris

Extensor Digiti Minimi

Gluteus Maximus

Vastus Lateralis

Gracilis

Semimembranosus

Biceps Femoris

Semitendinosus

Gastrocnemius

Soleus

Printed in Great Britain
by Amazon

78684513R00061